WHY ARE MEN EXPECTED NOT TO CRY?

BENJAMIN SCOTT

Copyright © 2025 by Benjamin Scott
All rights reserved.

No part of this book or the cover may be reproduced, distributed, or transmitted in any form or by any electronic or mechanical means, including recording, scanning, or photocopying, without the express written consent of the publisher.

Introduction

Men are taught from an early age that crying is something to be avoided. Tears are seen as a sign of weakness, something that doesn't belong in the world of strong, capable men. Whether it's a boy scraping his knee or a grown man facing heartbreak, the message is often the same, hold it in, stay strong, don't let anyone see you break.

But what if everything we've been told about emotions and masculinity is wrong? What if the ability to express pain, fear, and even joy isn't a weakness, but a strength? The truth is, suppressing emotions doesn't make them go away, it just buries them deeper. And over time, that emotional silence turns into stress, strained relationships, and a sense of loneliness that many men struggle to explain.

This book isn't about encouraging men to cry at every inconvenience or forcing emotions where they don't belong. It's about understanding why men have been expected to stay silent for so long and how that expectation has shaped their lives, often in ways they don't even realize. It's about breaking free from outdated ideas and learning that true strength isn't about how much you can endure without breaking, but how willing you are to face what's really going on inside.

If you've ever found yourself struggling to put your feelings into words, avoiding tough conversations, or feeling pressure to always keep it together, this book is for you. It's not about changing who you are, it's about giving yourself the freedom to be fully human.

Because at the end of the day, men feel just as deeply as anyone else. The real question is, why should they be expected to hide it?

TABLE OF CONTENTS

- Introduction..
1. The Boy Who Never Wept 1
2. Growing Up Without Tears 4
3. Lessons from Society............................... 7
4. The Father-Son Disconnect..................... 10
5. Cultural Pressures................................... 14
6. The Hidden Cost of Silence 17
7. Mental Health and Emotional Repression 21
8. The Physical cost of Bottled Emotions 24
9. Struggles in relationships 28
10. The loneliness of a stoic life 32
11. Redefining Strength 36
12. The healing power of crying............... 40
13. Getting help when you need it.......... 44
14. Mending broken bonds....................... 48
15. Tears Are Human 52
16. The Man Worth Looking Upto........... 56
17. The Strength in Letting Go 60
18. Changing ideas about masculinity 64
19. Raising emotionally aware boys 68
    - A Word from the Author

1. The Boy Who Never Wept

From the moment we're born, emotions are our first language. We cry to communicate hunger, discomfort, or fear before we even learn words. But somewhere along the way, for many boys, this natural expression of emotion is stifled. "Big boys don't cry," they hear. With that simple sentence, the foundation is laid for a lifetime of emotional suppression.

For many boys, the message starts subtly. A scraped knee is met with a stern "shake it off." Tears over a broken toy are dismissed with a curt "it's not a big deal." These responses, though often well-meaning, send a powerful signal: emotions, especially sadness or vulnerability, are not welcome.

As boys grow older, these lessons become more explicit. They learn that crying is a sign of weakness, a trait associated with women and children. Strength, they're told, lies in stoicism, silence in the face of pain. Over time, many boys internalize the belief that to be a man, they must suppress their emotions, even when it hurts.

The effects of this emotional suppression often manifest early. Boys may struggle to articulate their feelings, resorting instead to anger or withdrawal. Frustration becomes their default response, as it's one of the few emotions society permits them to express. Over time, this limited emotional vocabulary can hinder their ability to connect with others, leading to misunderstandings and strained relationships.

For instance, a boy who feels hurt by a friend's teasing might lash out instead of expressing his pain. A teenager grieving the loss of a loved one might retreat into isolation, unable to process their sorrow openly. These patterns, established in childhood, often follow men into adulthood, shaping their interactions and relationships.

Parents, teachers, and other authority figures play a significant role in perpetuating or challenging these norms. Unfortunately, many caregivers unconsciously reinforce the idea that boys must be tough. A father might tell his son to "man up" without realizing the long-term impact of those words. A teacher might praise a boy for "being strong" while discouraging him from showing vulnerability.

Understanding the roots of emotional suppression is the first step toward change. It's crucial to acknowledge that these societal norms didn't emerge overnight, they've been passed down through generations. Recognizing this allows men to begin questioning the beliefs they've been taught and exploring healthier ways to engage with their emotions.

2. Growing Up Without Tears

From the moment a boy learns to walk, he is met with expectations about how to act, what to say, and most importantly, what not to do. Crying, the most natural reaction to pain or frustration, quickly becomes one of the first behaviors boys are taught to suppress.

The process starts early. A toddler crying over a minor injury may be told, "You're fine, stop crying." While the intention might be to comfort or reassure, the message received is that tears are unnecessary. As boys grow older, the reprimands grow firmer. "Be a man" becomes a refrain they hear time and time again, long before they even understand what "being a man" really means.

These lessons don't just come from words. Boys observe the world around them. They notice that their sisters may be comforted when they cry, while they are encouraged to "tough it out." They see men in their lives who rarely, if ever, show vulnerability. From media to family dynamics, the examples they absorb reinforce the idea that masculinity and emotional restraint go hand in hand.

The shift away from tears often feels isolating. A boy who has been told to stop crying may not know how to replace this natural outlet. He may feel frustration building inside but lack the tools to express it. Over time, frustration becomes anger and sadness morphs into withdrawal. The emotions don't disappear, they simply take different shapes, often harder ones, that are more difficult to understand and manage.

As boys enter adolescence, the stakes grow higher. The social expectations around them tighten. A teenager who cries in front of his peers risks being teased or ostracized. The fear of being labelled "weak" or "soft" becomes a powerful motivator, driving emotional suppression even deeper. By the time many boys reach adulthood, the habit of holding back tears is so ingrained that they no longer even consider crying a viable option.

This learned behavior comes at a cost. Without an outlet for their emotions, boys carry an invisible weight that can grow heavier with time. The bottled-up feelings may lead to stress, anxiety, or even physical symptoms like headaches and tension. For many, the absence of tears becomes a silent burden they don't know how to unload.

Yet, some moments break through even the strongest barriers. The loss of a loved one, a moment of overwhelming joy, or a deeply painful experience might bring tears to the surface. When this happens, many men feel a mix of relief and discomfort, relief from finally releasing pent-up emotion, and discomfort from breaking the rules they've internalized for so long.

Growing up without tears shapes more than just emotional habits; it shapes identity. For many boys, the pressure to suppress emotions becomes a defining part of who they believe they are. Undoing this conditioning requires unlearning years of messages and embracing the idea that vulnerability is not a weakness but a strength.

3. Lessons from Society

Society has a way of teaching without words. From the shows we watch to the casual remarks we hear, it reinforces unspoken rules about how we're supposed to live, act, and feel. For boys, one of the clearest lessons they absorb is that emotions, especially those that make them appear vulnerable, are not acceptable.

This lesson is everywhere. Movies, for instance, depict heroes as stoic figures who weather pain and loss without shedding a tear. The few times male characters do cry, it's usually shown as an extraordinary moment, not an ordinary human experience. Boys grow up idolizing these characters, internalizing the idea that real men stay in control, no matter the circumstances.

At school, the message is echoed in the playground and the classroom. A boy who cries after losing a game or being teased might find himself the target of ridicule. Phrases like "man up" and "stop acting like a girl" are thrown around casually, not just by peers but sometimes by adults too. Each instance reinforces the idea that emotions, particularly sadness, are a liability, a weakness to overcome.

The workforce adds another layer to this conditioning. Professional environments often reward stoicism. The ideal worker is someone who can handle stress without complaint, take criticism without flinching, and push through challenges without showing cracks in their demeanor. Boys, aware of these expectations even before they enter adulthood, begin preparing themselves early. They learn to bury their feelings to fit into a world that seems to demand strength over sensitivity.

Cultural norms also play a significant role. In many cultures, men are expected to be the protectors and providers, roles that leave little room for vulnerability. A man who cries might be seen as shirking his responsibilities or failing to live up to these deeply ingrained ideals. These cultural expectations, passed down through generations, create a collective pressure that is hard to escape.

Even well-meaning advice can reinforce these lessons. Parents and mentors who want to prepare boys for a tough world might unintentionally teach them to suppress their emotions. "Stay strong" and "don't let them see you sweat" may come from a place of love, but they contribute to the larger narrative that emotions are something to hide.

Over time, these societal lessons shape how men view themselves and others. They may start to equate vulnerability with weakness, not just in themselves but in those around them. This mindset can lead to strained relationships, misunderstandings, and an inability to connect on a deeper level.

The irony is that society often celebrates emotional expression in other contexts. Artists, poets, and writers who lay their feelings bare are admired for their bravery. Yet, for the average man, the act of openly expressing emotion remains fraught with judgment and stigma.

4. The Father-Son Disconnect

For many boys, their father is the first and most influential male role model they have. Fathers often represent the ideals of masculinity that their sons look up to and want to emulate. However, in many families, a significant emotional gap exists between fathers and their sons, leaving young boys unsure of how to process their feelings. This gap can have long-lasting effects on how they approach relationships and emotional expression in adulthood.

One major reason for this emotional disconnect is the generational cycle of emotional suppression. Many fathers grew up in households where they were taught that emotions were a weakness. They were told not to cry, not to show vulnerability, and to always appear strong and in control. This mentality was passed down from their own fathers, and now, as adults, many of these men struggle to express their feelings or to encourage their sons to open up emotionally. Instead of having open conversations about their emotions, father-son relationships often rely on unspoken understandings and actions. This lack of communication creates a barrier between father and son, leaving both feeling isolated in their emotional experiences.

When a father avoids showing emotions, his son might feel alone, even in moments when he desperately needs comfort. A boy who is hurting or confused may hear phrases like "You'll be fine," or may be met with silence. While the intention behind these words might be to teach strength or to toughen the boy up, it often sends a harmful message; that emotions are not important and shouldn't be dealt with openly. Over time, this message becomes internalized, and the son learns to hide his feelings, just as his father did. This emotional distance can create lasting scars, especially if the boy feels like he is being rejected by his father, without realizing that his father may be struggling with his own inability to express himself.

This emotional gap in father-son relationships doesn't always look like silence. Sometimes, fathers may channel their feelings into teaching "tough love," focusing more on discipline, self-reliance, and toughness than on emotional openness. While lessons on responsibility and strength are valuable, they can also reinforce the belief that emotions are a weakness to be overcome. The son may grow up believing that showing any sign of vulnerability or emotion is something to avoid at all costs, even though these feelings are a natural and healthy part of being human.

Despite the challenges that this generational cycle of emotional suppression presents, there is hope for change. Fathers who recognize the importance of emotional openness can begin to model healthier behaviors for their sons, showing them that strength and vulnerability are not mutually exclusive. For example, a father who admits to making a mistake, expresses sadness, or openly shares a personal struggle can create a space where his son feels safe to do the same. These small acts can have a powerful impact, creating a deeper connection and a more meaningful relationship between father and son.

But this change doesn't rest solely on the shoulders of fathers. Sons also have a role to play in breaking the cycle. As adults, sons can take the initiative to have conversations with their fathers, seeking to understand their experiences and the pressures they faced growing up. These talks might be difficult, and it may take time for both sides to feel comfortable opening up.

Change in the father-son relationship doesn't rest solely on fathers. Sons, too, have an important role in breaking the cycle. By taking the first step to have conversations with their fathers, seeking to understand their experiences, and exploring the pressures their fathers faced while growing up, sons can begin to uncover generational patterns. These talks may not always be easy, but they open the door to healing and connection. Though it may take time, both fathers and sons can work together to overcome the emotional disconnect that has shaped their relationship for generations.

5. Cultural Pressures

From an early age, boys are immersed in cultural expectations that shape their understanding of strength and masculinity. These pressures are so deeply ingrained that they often go unnoticed, subtly guiding how men think, act, and feel throughout their lives.

The idea of strength in many cultures is tied to silence, toughness, and the ability to endure hardship without complaint. Boys are praised for "being strong" when they don't cry or show vulnerability, and they quickly learn that emotional expression is seen as a weakness. This belief is reinforced by stories, traditions, and media that celebrate stoic heroes who face challenges without shedding a tear.

In some cultures, these expectations are even more rigid. Men are seen as protectors and providers, roles that leave little room for vulnerability. A man who openly expresses sadness or fear might be labelled as weak or unfit for these responsibilities. This can create a significant internal conflict for boys and men who feel emotions deeply but are expected to hide them.

The pressure to appear strong doesn't just come from adults or authority figures. Peer groups also play a powerful role in shaping behavior. Boys often police each other's expressions of emotion, teasing or shaming those who step outside the accepted norms. A boy who cries in front of his friends might be called "soft" or told to "man up." These interactions reinforce the idea that fitting in means keeping emotions under control.

Media and entertainment add another layer to these cultural pressures. Movies, TV shows, and advertisements often portray men as stoic and unshakable, even in the face of loss or pain. When male characters do show emotion, it's usually in extreme or exceptional situations, reinforcing the idea that vulnerability is the exception rather than the rule.

These cultural pressures have significant consequences. Men who grow up believing they must always be strong may struggle to recognize or accept their own emotions. They might avoid seeking help when they need it, fearing judgment or rejection. Over time, this suppression can lead to stress, anxiety, and even physical health problems.

Despite these challenges, cultural norms are not set in stone. Over time, they can evolve. In recent years, there has been a growing movement to challenge traditional ideas of masculinity and redefine what it means to be strong. More men are speaking openly about their emotions, sharing their struggles, and showing that vulnerability is a form of courage.

6. The Hidden Cost of Silence

For many men, staying silent about their emotions feels like the safest choice. It's easier to keep things inside than to risk judgment or appear vulnerable. Over time, though, this silence comes with a cost, a price that often remains hidden until it becomes too heavy to ignore.

When emotions are bottled up, they don't disappear; they build up, often beneath the surface, where they can fester. Frustration, sadness, and even joy that goes unexpressed can create tension within, leading to stress and emotional exhaustion. The effort to appear strong on the outside while struggling internally can leave men feeling drained, disconnected and alone.

One of the most significant costs of silence is its impact on mental health. Suppressing emotions can contribute to feelings of anxiety and depression. Without an outlet, negative emotions can spiral, leaving men feeling overwhelmed but unable to articulate what they're going through.

Take, for example, James, a 35-year-old father of two. James always prided himself on being the steady one in his family, never showing weakness or stress. But when he lost his job, the pressure of keeping it together became unbearable. Instead of opening up to his wife or friends, he withdrew, spending hours alone in silence. His unspoken frustration and sadness eventually turned into depression, making it harder for him to find solutions or connect with those who wanted to support him.

In some cases, this silence becomes a barrier to seeking help. For men like James, admitting to struggling can feel like failing. This mindset prevents many men from accessing therapy or support groups, leaving them to deal with their pain in isolation.

The physical effects of emotional suppression are just as real. Stress from unspoken emotions can manifest as headaches, tension, fatigue, or even more serious health problems like high blood pressure, ulcers, or heart issues.

Consider Mike, a 40-year-old manager at a high-pressure job. Mike rarely spoke about how overwhelmed he felt, even when the demands at work kept piling up. He began experiencing constant tension headaches, but instead of addressing the root cause, his stress. He popped painkillers and pushed through. Eventually, Mike's doctor warned him that his skyrocketing blood pressure was putting him at risk for a heart attack.

Silence can also take a toll on relationships. Partners, friends, and family members may struggle to connect with someone who doesn't share their feelings. Misunderstandings can arise, with loved ones interpreting silence as disinterest or detachment. Over time, this emotional distance can erode trust and intimacy, making meaningful connections harder to maintain.

For example, Ethan's wife often told him she felt like she didn't really know him. When she asked how he was feeling, his default response was "I'm fine." Over time, her frustration grew, and she began to feel disconnected from the man she loved. Ethan's silence, meant to protect her from his worries, ended up creating a rift in their marriage.

Yet, the cost of silence isn't inevitable. Breaking this pattern starts with small steps, acknowledging emotions, finding someone to talk to, or even writing feelings down. Expressing emotions doesn't have to mean losing control;

it's about finding ways to release them in a healthy and constructive manner.

For James, it meant opening up to his wife and starting therapy. For Mike, it meant learning stress management techniques and setting boundaries at work. For Ethan, it meant listening to his wife's concerns and learning how to communicate his feelings, even when it felt uncomfortable.

7. Mental Health and Emotional Repression

Mental health is a topic that many people shy away from, especially men. For years, men have been conditioned to "push through" difficult emotions and handle life's challenges without showing signs of struggle. But repressing emotions doesn't make them disappear, it buries them, and over time, this emotional repression can have serious consequences on mental health.

Imagine carrying a heavy backpack everywhere you go. At first, it might not seem like a big deal. You adjust to the weight and keep moving. But as you add more to the bag, stress, sadness, frustration, it becomes harder to carry. Eventually, that weight slows you down, and you can't move forward without dealing with it. This is what emotional repression does to mental health, it builds up until it becomes impossible to ignore.

Repressed emotions often lead to anxiety and depression. When feelings are bottled up, they don't have an outlet, so they manifest in other ways. A man who struggles with sadness might find himself constantly irritable or angry, snapping at others over minor things. Another man dealing with fear or self-doubt might withdraw from social situations, choosing isolation over the risk of vulnerability.

Take Ryan, for example, a 32-year-old sales professional. Ryan always prided himself on being calm and collected, no matter what life threw at him. But after a difficult breakup, he refused to talk about how he felt. He distracted himself with work, avoided his friends, and convinced himself he was "fine." Months later, he started having trouble sleeping, and small tasks felt overwhelming. Ryan didn't realize that his refusal to process his emotions was fuelling his anxiety.

The stigma around mental health often makes it harder for men to address these struggles. Many men grow up believing that seeking help is a sign of weakness, so they try to handle everything on their own. This mindset can prevent them from talking to a trusted friend, let alone a therapist. The result is a cycle where problems go unaddressed, leading to more stress, loneliness, and a deeper sense of hopelessness.

Another common result of emotional repression is self-medication. Many men turn to alcohol, drugs, or other unhealthy coping mechanisms to numb the pain they can't express. While these behaviors might provide temporary relief, they often make the underlying issues worse. Instead of facing their emotions, men end up adding another layer of problems to their lives.

The good news is that this cycle can be broken. Addressing mental health doesn't have to be overwhelming or complicated. It starts with small steps, like acknowledging how you feel and giving yourself permission to experience emotions without judgment.

For Ryan, the turning point came when a close friend noticed he wasn't himself and encouraged him to talk. At first, Ryan hesitated, worried about being seen as weak. But opening up about his struggles was a relief, and it helped him realize he wasn't alone. Eventually, Ryan decided to see a therapist, where he learned healthy ways to process his emotions and manage his anxiety.

8. The Physical cost of Bottled Emotions

When emotions are buried instead of expressed, they don't just affect the mind, they take a toll on the body, too. Many men underestimate how much their unspoken feelings can impact their physical health. But the connection between emotions and the body is powerful, and ignoring it can lead to serious consequences.

Stress is one of the most obvious ways suppressed emotions show up in the body. When emotions are bottled up, the body stays on high alert, producing stress hormones like cortisol. Over time, this constant state of tension can cause headaches, muscle pain, and fatigue. It's like keeping your foot on the gas pedal of a car without ever letting up, it eventually wears out the engine.

Take Sam, a 38-year-old construction worker. Sam prided himself on being tough and never letting anything bother him. But over the years, he noticed he was always tired and dealing with constant back pain. Despite visiting doctors and trying various treatments, nothing seemed to help. It wasn't until Sam opened up to a friend about the stress of balancing work and family that he realized his physical pain wasn't just about his body, it was connected to the stress he had been ignoring for years.

Chronic stress can lead to more serious health problems, such as high blood pressure, heart disease, and even digestive issues. For men who avoid processing their emotions, these physical symptoms often act as warning signs that something deeper needs attention. Unfortunately, many ignore these signs, choosing to push through the pain instead of addressing the root cause.

The immune system also takes a hit when emotions are repressed. Studies show that stress and emotional suppression can weaken the body's ability to fight off illness. Men who suppress their feelings may find themselves getting sick more often or taking longer to recover from illnesses. This isn't just a coincidence, it's the body reacting to the weight of unprocessed emotions.

Sleep is another area that often suffers. Men who suppress their emotions may struggle with insomnia, restless nights, or frequent waking. Lying in bed, their minds race with thoughts they've been avoiding during the day. Without proper rest, the body doesn't get the chance to repair itself, leading to a cycle of exhaustion and poor health.

For some men, emotional suppression can also lead to harmful coping mechanisms. They might turn to alcohol, smoking, or overeating as a way to numb their feelings. While these habits may provide temporary relief, they often worsen physical health in the long run, adding another layer of strain to the body.

Breaking this cycle starts with recognizing the connection between emotions and physical health. It's not about becoming overly emotional or expressing every thought rather, it's about finding healthy outlets for feelings before they take a toll on the body.

For Sam, that meant finding ways to manage his stress and talk about his struggles. He started going for regular walks to clear his mind. He also began opening up to his wife, which helped him feel less alone in dealing with his challenges. Over time, his back pain began to ease, and he noticed an overall improvement in his energy and mood.

Exercise and relaxation techniques can help release built-up tension in the body. Activities like yoga or meditation, for example, can help calm the mind and reduce stress hormones. Even something as simple as taking deep breaths during a tense moment can make a big difference.

Listening to your body is crucial. If you notice recurring pain, fatigue, or other physical symptoms, take a step back and consider whether unprocessed emotions might be a factor. Your body is often the first to signal when something is wrong, and paying attention to those signals can help you act before it's too late.

9. Struggles in relationships

Relationships thrive on connection, trust, and communication, but when emotions are hidden or left unspoken, even the strongest relationships can struggle. For many men, the difficulty in expressing feelings becomes a barrier to forming deep, meaningful connections with their partners, family and friends.

Take Mark, for example, a 34-year-old who had been married for five years. Mark loved his wife deeply, but whenever they had a disagreement, he would shut down. Instead of talking about what was bothering him, he'd say, "It's fine," and brush it off. Over time, his wife grew frustrated. She felt like she couldn't reach him emotionally and Mark started feeling distant in his own marriage. He didn't realize that by avoiding his emotions, he was unintentionally creating a wall between them.

This pattern is common. Many men grow up learning to suppress their emotions, so when it comes to relationships, they struggle to share their feelings or even recognize what they're feeling. While their intention might be to avoid conflict or seem strong, this emotional silence often leads to misunderstandings, resentment, and a lack of intimacy.

Partners may misinterpret this silence as indifference or disinterest. A wife might think her husband doesn't care about her feelings, or a friend might feel like they're the only one putting effort into the relationship. This imbalance can create tension, even if the man deeply values the relationship.

Friendships can also suffer. Many men form friendships based on shared activities rather than emotional support. While this type of bond is valuable, it often lacks the depth to handle life's tougher moments. A man going through a hard time might hesitate to open up to his friends, fearing judgment or ridicule. Instead, he keeps his struggles to himself, missing the chance to lean on those who care about him.

In families, the struggles are similar. A father who doesn't express his emotions may find it hard to connect with his children on a deeper level. Sons might grow up feeling that emotions are a weakness, while daughters may feel their father is distant or unapproachable. This emotional gap can persist for years, creating strained relationships that feel more like obligations than meaningful connections.

The impact of emotional suppression on relationships isn't just one-sided. Men often feel isolated in their silence, longing for connection but unsure of how to bridge the gap. The fear of being vulnerable or saying the wrong thing can hold them back, leading to frustration and loneliness.

Breaking this cycle starts with small but meaningful steps. For Mark, it began with admitting to his wife that he struggled to talk about his feelings. Instead of trying to solve every problem on his own, he started sharing his thoughts, even when it felt uncomfortable. Over time, their communication improved, and the emotional distance between them began to shrink.

Learning to express emotions doesn't mean turning every conversation into a therapy session. It's about being honest and open in small ways, saying, "I'm upset," instead of pretending everything is okay, or sharing a worry instead of holding it inside. These simple acts of vulnerability can inspire others to open up too.

In friendships, this might look like checking in on a friend who seems down or admitting when you're going through a tough time. True friends won't see vulnerability as weakness; they'll appreciate the trust and respond with support.

Within families, opening up can mean asking questions, sharing personal stories, or simply saying, "I love you," more often. These moments of emotional connection can strengthen bonds that might have felt distant or strained.

The truth is, relationships flourish when emotions are acknowledged, not ignored. By trying to share feelings and listen to others, men can build deeper connections and create a sense of closeness that transforms their relationships.

10. The loneliness of a stoic life

For many men, being strong means keeping emotions locked away. Society often teaches that a "real man" handles things on his own, without seeking help or showing vulnerability. But over time, this self-imposed isolation leads to something far heavier, loneliness.

Loneliness doesn't always look like being physically alone. A man can be surrounded by friends, have a family, or work in a busy office and still feel disconnected. The real issue isn't the lack of people around him, it's the absence of emotional connection. When a man spends years suppressing his emotions, avoiding difficult conversations, and keeping his struggles to himself, he creates a wall between himself and the people who care about him.

David, a 42-year-old business owner, had everything on paper, success, financial stability and a wide social circle. But deep down, he felt alone. He never talked about his fears or personal struggles, assuming no one wanted to hear them. Over time, his friendships became surface-level, his marriage felt distant, and despite being around people daily, he felt isolated. He thought he was protecting himself by not burdening others, but in reality, he was shutting people out.

Many men experience this same silent loneliness. They might go to social gatherings, joke with friends, or even be in long-term relationships, yet still feel unseen or unheard. The reason is simple, without emotional openness, relationships lack real depth.

Loneliness isn't just an emotional burden, it has real health consequences. Studies show that chronic loneliness can increase the risk of heart disease, high blood pressure, and even premature death. It also impacts mental health, leading to increased anxiety, stress, and depression. The burden of carrying everything alone slowly takes its toll.

One of the biggest challenges men face in breaking this cycle is the fear of rejection or judgment. Many worry that if they open up, they'll be seen as weak or that people won't care. This fear keeps them locked in a cycle where they crave connection but are too afraid to reach out for it.

The good news is that loneliness isn't permanent, it's something that can be changed with conscious effort. It starts with small steps, like being more open in conversations, reaching out to an old friend, or admitting when things aren't okay. Even a simple "Hey, I've been struggling with something" can be the first step in breaking years of emotional isolation.

For David, his turning point came when a close friend confided in him about a personal challenge. Seeing his friend open up without shame made David realize he wasn't alone in his struggles. He decided to take a chance and share his own feelings, and to his surprise, his friend listened without judgment. That one conversation led to deeper connections in his friendships and marriage, proving that vulnerability doesn't push people away, it brings them closer.

Building emotional connections doesn't mean oversharing with everyone. It's about identifying safe and trusted people to talk to, whether it's a close friend, a sibling, a partner, or even a therapist. Over time, these small moments of honesty create stronger, more fulfilling relationships.

Men don't have to carry the burden of the world alone. Loneliness is not a sign of failure, it's a signal that something needs to change. By allowing themselves to connect on a deeper level, men can find the support, understanding, and companionship they've been missing.

11. Redefining Strength

For most of their lives, men are taught that strength means being tough, unemotional, and always in control. Society praises the man who never complains, never cries, and never asks for help. He's the one who handles everything on his own, never showing signs of struggle. But is that really strength? Or is it just fear of being seen as weak?

Real strength isn't about hiding emotions, it's about having the courage to face them. It takes far more strength to be honest about struggles than to pretend they don't exist. A man who expresses his feelings, asks for help when needed, and supports others isn't weak, he's strong. Strength isn't about how much weight you can carry, but whether you have the wisdom to put some of it down when it gets too heavy.

Think about Jake, a 37-year-old firefighter. His job was all about bravery, facing life-threatening situations daily. But after losing a close colleague in an accident, Jake found himself struggling. He barely slept, felt constantly on edge, and started distancing himself from his wife and kids. He convinced himself that talking about his pain would make him seem weak, so he bottled it up. The more he kept it inside, the worse it got.

One day, another firefighter, someone he respected, shared his own struggles with mental health. That moment changed everything for Jake. He realized that even the strongest men feel pain, and true strength lies in dealing with it, not ignoring it. He started talking to a therapist and found that opening up made him feel lighter, not weaker. Instead of dragging his pain with him every day, he finally had a way to process it.

Many men believe strength means handling everything alone. They think being independent is the ultimate sign of masculinity. But no man is an island. Even the strongest warriors throughout history had trusted allies. A soldier relies on his team, a leader depends on his advisors, and an athlete succeeds with the support of a coach. True strength isn't about isolating yourself, it's about knowing when to lean on others.

Physical strength is easy to recognize, but emotional strength is just as important. It means staying true to yourself, admitting when you're struggling, and refusing to let fear dictate your actions. A strong man doesn't suppress his emotions, he manages them. He doesn't avoid difficult conversations, he faces them. He doesn't act like he has all the answers, he seeks help when he needs it.

One of the biggest misconceptions about masculinity is that vulnerability is a flaw. In reality, vulnerability is the gateway to deeper relationships, personal growth, and true confidence. A man who can say, "I need help" or "I'm struggling" is showing bravery, not weakness. It takes strength to admit you don't have everything figured out.

Tom, a 45-year-old father of three, learned this lesson the hard way. For years, he bottled up the stress of work and family responsibilities, thinking he had to be the rock everyone depended on. But that pressure built up, and one day, he snapped at his kids over something small. Seeing their hurt expressions, he realized that being emotionally closed off wasn't protecting them, it was pushing them away. That night, he finally sat down with his wife and talked honestly about his stress. Instead of judging him, she reassured him that he wasn't alone.

From that moment on, Tom started prioritizing his emotional health, realizing that being open with his family made him a better husband and father.

This shift in mindset isn't just beneficial for individuals, it impacts society as a whole. When men embrace a healthier definition of strength, they become better partners, fathers, friends and leaders. They create environments where younger generations of boys grow up understanding that emotions don't make them less of a man, they make them human.

Breaking free from outdated ideas of masculinity isn't easy, but it starts with small steps. It's about questioning old beliefs, allowing yourself to feel without shame, and recognizing that real strength is about resilience, not suppression. It's about knowing that reaching out for help doesn't mean you're weak, it means you're smart enough to recognize when you need support.

Strength isn't about never falling, it's about getting back up, time and time again, with the wisdom to know you don't have to do it alone.

12. The healing power of crying

Crying is one of the most natural human responses to pain, stress, or overwhelming emotions, yet for many men, it feels like a forbidden act. From childhood, boys are taught that tears are a sign of weakness, something to be ashamed of rather than embraced. Over time, this conditioning leads to men suppressing one of their body's most effective ways of releasing emotional tension.

Tears aren't just about sadness. People cry when they're frustrated, overwhelmed, relieved, or even deeply moved by something meaningful. It's the body's way of processing emotions, much like sweating helps cool the body down. Studies have shown that crying releases stress hormones and stimulates the production of endorphins, which can improve mood and provide a sense of relief.

Michael, a 40-year-old gym owner, had spent his entire life believing that men don't cry. He took pride in being strong, in pushing through pain without showing emotion. But when his father passed away, something changed. He tried to act as if everything was fine, but inside, his grief was unbearable. No matter how much he worked out or distracted himself, the pain wouldn't go away.

One night, while watching an old video of his father, he finally broke down. The tears came uncontrollably, and for the first time in months, he felt like he could breathe again. That moment made him realize that crying wasn't a sign of weakness, it was a release. The emotions he had been carrying for so long didn't feel as heavy after he allowed himself to let them out.

Despite its benefits, many men avoid crying at all costs. Some fear judgment from others, while others feel uncomfortable with the vulnerability that comes with it. But avoiding tears doesn't make emotions disappear, it only buries them deeper. Over time, suppressed feelings can turn into stress, anxiety, or even physical symptoms like headaches and fatigue.

Crying doesn't have to be a public act. Many men feel more comfortable letting their emotions out in private, whether it's during a moment of reflection, while listening to music, or after watching a powerful movie.

The key is allowing those emotions to surface rather than shutting them down the moment they arise.

For those who struggle with crying, starting small can help. Acknowledging emotions instead of immediately pushing them away is the first step. Writing in a journal, talking to someone trusted, or even sitting with emotions instead of distracting from them can create space for release.

In relationships, allowing tears can deepen emotional bonds. A man who is open about his feelings is often seen as more trustworthy and relatable. Many women express frustration when their male partners shut down emotionally, not because they want them to be overly sensitive, but because emotional openness fosters connection.

In cultures where men crying is still stigmatized, it's important to challenge outdated beliefs. Many of history's greatest leaders, athletes, and warriors have shed tears without losing respect. True strength isn't about avoiding emotions, it's about having the courage to feel them fully.

Crying isn't a weakness. It's a form of healing. It helps clear emotional blockages, reduces stress, and allows the mind and body to reset. Whether it's grief, frustration, or joy, letting emotions flow instead of forcing them down is a powerful step toward emotional well-being.

Men don't have to cry to be emotionally healthy, but they do need to stop fearing it. Tears aren't the problem, hiding from emotions is. Once men understand that, they can start embracing a fuller, more authentic version of themselves.

13. Getting help when you need it

Many men grow up believing they have to handle everything on their own. Whether it's stress, emotional struggles, or personal problems, they are taught that asking for help is a sign of weakness. The idea of "figuring it out yourself" is deeply ingrained in male culture, leading many to suffer in silence rather than seek support.

James, a 36-year-old mechanic, had always been the guy who others depended on. At work, he was the go-to problem solver. At home, he was the one holding everything together. But when he started feeling constantly exhausted and overwhelmed, he didn't know what to do. He told himself to "push through it," convinced that asking for help would mean admitting failure. The more he ignored his struggles, the worse they got. His frustration grew, his patience ran thin, and even small problems started to feel impossible.

One evening, his wife sat him down and said, "I know something's wrong, but you won't talk about it. You don't have to do this alone." That conversation changed everything. For the first time, James admitted to himself that he was struggling. He reached out to a friend and eventually spoke to a therapist. What he feared would make him look weak actually made him feel stronger. By getting help, he started finding real solutions instead of just carrying the weight alone.

One of the biggest barriers men face in asking for help is, the fear of judgment. Society has conditioned men to believe they should always be in control, that needing support makes them less capable. But the truth is, everyone struggles at some point. No one gets through life without needing guidance, whether it's from a friend, a mentor, or a professional.

Getting help doesn't always mean seeing a counsellor, though that can be incredibly beneficial. Sometimes, it's as simple as opening up to a trusted friend or family member. Just saying the words "I'm struggling" can be a powerful first step. Other times, it might mean seeking advice from someone who's been through similar challenges or joining a support group where people understand what you're going through.

Many men think their problems aren't "big enough" to warrant help. They assume that unless they're completely falling apart, they should just deal with things on their own. But struggles come in all sizes, and waiting until things are unbearable only makes them harder to fix. The sooner a problem is addressed, the easier it is to manage.

For those unsure of where to start, small steps can make a big difference. Reaching out to a close friend, writing down thoughts to process emotions, or even reading about others who have faced similar struggles can help. If professional help feels intimidating, consider online resources or helplines where support is available without pressure.

Getting help isn't about giving up control, it's about gaining it. When men act to improve their mental and emotional well-being, they become stronger, not weaker. They show courage by facing challenges head-on instead of ignoring them.

James learned that asking for help didn't change who he was, it just made him better at handling life. His relationships improved, his stress became manageable, and for the first time in years, he felt lighter. The problems didn't disappear overnight, but he no longer had to carry them alone.

No one is meant to handle everything by themselves. Strength isn't about suffering in silence, it's about knowing when to reach out. The moment a man realizes that, he takes his first step toward real freedom.

14. Mending broken bonds

Relationships can be complicated, and over time, misunderstandings, pride, or emotional distance can create gaps between people who once shared a strong connection. Many men find themselves in situations where a friendship has faded, a family relationship has become strained, or a romantic partnership feels distant. When bonds break, it's easy to assume they're beyond repair, but that's rarely the case.

Ethan, a 39-year-old father of two, hadn't spoken to his younger brother in nearly five years. What started as a small argument over a family issue turned into complete silence between them. Both assumed the other didn't care enough to fix things, and with time, the distance only grew. Even though Ethan missed his brother, he didn't know how to reach out. He told himself, "If he cared, he'd call me first."

This kind of thinking is common. Many men struggle with repairing relationships because they see apologizing or making the first move as a loss of pride. But in reality, taking the first step isn't a sign of weakness, it's a sign of strength. Holding onto grudges or waiting for the other person to reach out only deepens the divide.

Mending a broken bond starts with honesty. It means recognizing what went wrong and being willing to address it. Sometimes, the issue is a misunderstanding that was never cleared up. Other times, it might be deeper, involving hurt feelings, trust issues, or emotional distance. Regardless of the cause, healing begins with a conversation.

For some men, expressing emotions can feel uncomfortable, especially when it comes to repairing relationships. The fear of rejection or awkwardness can make it easier to just ignore the issue. But in the long run, avoiding the problem only leads to regret. Many men look back and wish they had reached out before it was too late.

When Ethan finally decided to call his brother, he didn't have a big speech planned. He simply said, "I know it's been a long time, and I miss you. I don't want whatever happened between us to keep us apart any longer." To his surprise, his brother felt the same way. Neither of them cared about the original argument anymore, they had just been waiting for the other to make the first move.

Not every situation will be resolved that easily, but most broken relationships can be repaired if both people are willing. If direct conversation feels too difficult at first, writing a message or even sending a simple "Hey, I've been thinking about you" can open the door. The goal isn't to have a perfect, scripted discussion, it's to break the silence.

Sometimes, an apology is needed. Owning up to past mistakes or acknowledging someone's hurt feelings can be difficult, but it's one of the most powerful ways to rebuild trust. A genuine "I'm sorry for how things turned out" can go a long way.

There will be cases where the other person isn't ready to mend the bond, and that's okay. Repairing relationships takes time, and not everyone will be open to reconnecting immediately. The important thing is making the effort and knowing that you tried.

Fixing broken relationships doesn't mean dwelling on the past, it means moving forward. Whether it's a friendship, a family bond, or a romantic relationship, taking the first step can bring back the connection that was once lost.

Ethan and his brother may have lost years, but by choosing to reconnect, they made sure they wouldn't lose any more.

No relationship is perfect, and every bond will face challenges. But with effort, patience, and a willingness to reach out, even the most broken relationships can be restored.

15. Tears Are Human

From an early age, many men are taught that crying is something to be ashamed of. Boys who cry are often told to "toughen up" or "stop acting like a girl," reinforcing the belief that real men don't show emotion. Over time, this message becomes deeply ingrained, making men see tears as a sign of weakness rather than a natural human response.

But the truth is, crying is not a weakness, it's a release. It's the body's way of handling overwhelming emotions, just like sweating helps cool the body or breathing deeply helps calm the mind. Scientists have even found that tears contain stress hormones, meaning crying is literally a way to cleanse the body of built-up tension.

Nathan, a 41-year-old former athlete, had spent his entire life avoiding tears. Growing up, his father always told him to "be strong" whenever he got hurt or felt sad. As an adult, Nathan carried this mindset into his career and relationships. Even when he lost his best friend to illness, he held everything in, refusing to cry. He thought staying composed was a sign of control, but inside, the grief weighed on him.

Months later, while driving alone, a song on the radio triggered a flood of memories. Without warning, tears came rushing down his face. He pulled over, feeling embarrassed at first, but as he let himself cry, something changed. He felt lighter, as if a pressure that had been building for months had finally been released. That moment made him realize that crying wasn't weakness, it was necessary.

Men often fear that crying will make them look fragile or less masculine. But some of the strongest men in history, leaders, warriors, and athletes, have shed tears in times of hardship, loss, and even triumph. Tears don't make a man less capable; they make him human.

Suppressing emotions doesn't make them disappear. When men force themselves to hold back tears, the stress and sadness don't go away, they just get buried deeper. Over time, this can lead to anxiety, anger, or even physical symptoms like headaches and muscle tension. What starts as "staying strong" can turn into a silent battle with stress and frustration.

Crying isn't something that has to be done in front of others. Many men feel more comfortable letting their emotions out in private, whether it's during a quiet moment at home, while watching a meaningful movie, or when reflecting on a personal experience. The important thing is allowing emotions to flow rather than shutting them down.

In relationships, showing emotion can actually strengthen connections. When a man allows himself to be vulnerable, his partner, friends, or family see him as more genuine and trustworthy. Many women, in particular, express frustration when their male partners hide emotions, not because they want them to be overly sensitive, but because openness creates deeper intimacy and understanding.

Changing the mindset around tears doesn't happen overnight. It starts with recognizing that emotions aren't a problem to be fixed, they're a natural part of being alive. A man who allows himself to feel is not weak, he's self-aware. He's not losing control, he's taking care of his mental and emotional well-being.

Nathan never became someone who cried often, but he no longer saw tears as something to avoid. He understood that when emotions became overwhelming, letting them out wasn't just okay, it was healthy. He no longer judged himself for feeling deeply, and in doing so, he became more in touch with himself and those around him.

Crying isn't a sign of failure. It's proof that you're alive, that you care, and that you feel. Tears don't make a man weak, they make him human.

16. The Man Worth Upto

For generations, men have been taught to admire the strong, silent type, the kind of man who never shows fear, never cries, and never lets emotions get in the way. This idea of masculinity has shaped how boys grow up, how men handle struggles, and how they define success. But this version of strength has left many men feeling trapped, unable to express their real emotions for fear of looking weak.

It's time to redefine what it means to be a man worth looking up to. The world doesn't need more emotionless, distant figures, it needs men who are both strong and self-aware. Men who don't just endure hardship but grow from it. Men who understand that real strength isn't about hiding struggles but about facing them head-on.

Take Daniel, a 35-year-old father of two. He grew up in a home where his dad never talked about feelings. When things got tough, his father would retreat into silence or anger. Daniel followed the same pattern for years, never opening up about his struggles. But when he noticed his own son shutting down whenever he was upset, something clicked. He realized he was passing down the same emotional avoidance he had learned. That was the moment he decided to be different. He started having real conversations with his son, showing him that expressing emotions wasn't a weakness but a way to handle life better.

This is what a man worth looking up to does, he leads by example. Not by pretending to be invincible, but by showing that emotional strength is just as important as physical or mental toughness. He isn't afraid to say, "I don't have all the answers," or "I need help," because he knows that admitting struggle is the first step toward growth.

Role models don't have to be celebrities, athletes, or larger-than-life figures. They can be the mentor who encourages young men to express themselves, the husband who listens instead of shutting down, or the friend who checks in when he notices someone pulling away. These everyday examples are more powerful than any famous figure because they are real, personal, and within reach.

Aaron, a 42-year-old business owner, used to believe that handling stress alone was part of being a man. He never shared his problems with his wife, believing it was his job to be strong for the family. But the more he suppressed his worries, the more distant he became. Eventually, his wife told him, "I don't need you to have all the answers, I just need to know what's going on in your head." That moment changed everything. He realized that by opening up, he wasn't burdening his family, he was strengthening his connection with them.

A man worth looking up to is someone who embraces balance. He knows that being strong and being vulnerable are not opposites. He understands that resilience doesn't mean avoiding emotions but learning how to manage them. He values independence but also recognizes the power of connection.

Men today have the opportunity to redefine masculinity, not by rejecting strength, but by expanding its meaning. By being open, honest, and emotionally present, they set an example for the next generation, showing boys that being a man isn't about shutting down, it's about stepping up in every way.

A real man is not the one who feels nothing, he's the one who feels everything and still keeps going. That's the kind of man worth looking up to.

17. The Strength in Letting Go

Many men grow up believing that strength means holding everything together, never breaking, never asking for help, and never letting go. Whether it's stress, past mistakes, or the pressure to meet expectations, the idea is that real men carry their burdens alone. But over time, this weight becomes exhausting. The truth is, real strength isn't about holding on to everything, it's about knowing when to let go.

Letting go doesn't mean giving up or becoming weak. It means freeing yourself from things that no longer serve you, unrealistic expectations, emotional burdens, past regrets, or the need to always be in control. Holding onto these things doesn't make a man stronger; it only weighs him down.

Take Jake, a 38-year-old paramedic. His job required him to be tough under pressure, and for years, he believed that showing emotion made him weak. He saw things most people never had to witness, accidents, emergencies, life-or-death situations. To cope, he built a wall around his emotions, convincing himself that shutting down was the only way to stay strong.

At home, his wife noticed the change. He stopped talking about his day, withdrew from conversations, and became distant. His kids saw him as "the strong dad," but they rarely saw him express anything real. The more he suppressed his emotions, the heavier they became.

One night, after responding to a particularly difficult call, Jake sat in his car and felt something he hadn't allowed himself to feel in years, overwhelming sadness. For the first time, he let himself cry. He realized that holding everything in wasn't making him stronger, it was breaking him. That night, he decided. He reached out to a co-worker who had been through something similar. Talking about it didn't erase the pain, but it made it lighter. He finally understood that strength wasn't about bottling everything up, it was about facing emotions and letting go of the ones that no longer served him.

Letting go can mean different things for different men. Sometimes, it means forgiving yourself for past mistakes instead of carrying guilt for years. Other times, it means letting go of the need to always be right in a relationship and choosing connection over pride. It can mean walking away from toxic friendships, releasing unrealistic pressures, or finally admitting that you can't do everything alone.

Daniel, a 45-year-old business owner, spent years believing that his worth was tied to his success. He worked long hours, built a thriving company, and sacrificed time with his family to maintain his business. But no matter how much he achieved, he never felt like it was enough. The stress became unbearable, yet he refused to slow down.

His turning point came when his health started to decline, constant headaches, exhaustion, and anxiety that he could no longer ignore. He finally realized that success at the cost of his well-being wasn't worth it. Letting go, for him, meant releasing the pressure to prove himself and prioritizing what truly mattered, his health and his relationships.

Letting go doesn't happen overnight. It's a process of unlearning old beliefs and replacing them with healthier ones. It requires trust, trust in yourself, trust in others, and trust that releasing control doesn't mean losing it.

A man who can let go of what weighs him down isn't weak, he's free. He understands that real strength isn't about holding everything in but about knowing what to release. By letting go of unnecessary burdens, men create space for peace, clarity, and real emotional strength.

Strength isn't about carrying the heaviest load, it's about knowing what's worth carrying at all.

18. Changing ideas about masculinity

For generations, men have been raised with a strict definition of masculinity, one built on toughness, independence, and emotional control. From childhood, they are taught to "be a man," "tough it out," and never show weakness. These messages shape how they see themselves and how they move through life. But as the world changes, so does the understanding of what it truly means to be a man.

Many men reach a point where they start questioning these old ideas. They wonder if staying silent about their struggles is really making them stronger or if carrying every burden alone is actually making life harder. They ask themselves why expressing emotions feels so unnatural and why seeking help still carries a sense of shame. The truth is, the traditional idea of masculinity often limits men more than it empowers them.

Take Ryan, a 33-year-old construction worker. He grew up in a family where men never talked about feelings. His father rarely showed emotion, and when

Ryan cried as a kid, he was told to "stop acting soft." As an adult, he followed the same pattern, handling stress by burying it, never admitting when he was struggling, and refusing to ask for help. On the outside, he seemed fine, but inside, the pressure kept building.

Everything changed when one of his closest friends opened up about his own struggles with anxiety. Instead of judging him, Ryan felt relief, he wasn't alone. That conversation made him realize that being open about emotions didn't make someone weak. It made them human.

Breaking free from old ideas of masculinity isn't about rejecting strength or toughness, it's about expanding the definition of what it means to be strong. A man can be both tough and compassionate, independent and connected, confident and vulnerable. Strength isn't just about endurance; it's also about self-awareness and emotional balance.

For many men, unlearning these outdated beliefs starts with small steps. It could be as simple as acknowledging when they are feeling overwhelmed instead of pretending everything is fine. It might mean reaching out to a friend, expressing frustration in a healthy way instead of bottling it up, or allowing themselves to grieve without shame.

In relationships, breaking free from old ideas can lead to deeper connections. Many men were taught that providing financially is their primary role in a family. While financial stability is important, being emotionally present matters just as much. A father who listens to his children, a husband who communicates openly with his wife, or a friend who offers real support instead of just advice, these are the men who redefine strength.

Workplace culture is also shifting. In the past, men were expected to push through stress without complaint, work long hours without question, and never admit to feeling overwhelmed. But more men are now recognizing that success doesn't have to come at the expense of mental health. Taking breaks, setting boundaries, and prioritizing well-being are no longer seen as signs of weakness, they are signs of wisdom.

For years, masculinity was defined in rigid terms, leaving little room for emotional expression or personal growth. But men today have the opportunity to rewrite that definition. They can choose to be strong in a way that isn't about hiding emotions but embracing them. They can be leaders who don't just command respect but earn it through authenticity.

Ryan eventually started making small changes. He allowed himself to talk more openly with his wife. He checked in on his friends instead of just talking about work or sports. He realized that being a man wasn't about following outdated rules, it was about being true to himself.

Real masculinity isn't about proving something to others. It's about living in a way that feels real, balanced, and fulfilling. The strongest men aren't the ones who never struggle, they are the ones who have the courage to grow.

19. Raising emotionally aware boys

The way boys are raised shapes the kind of men they become. For generations, boys were taught to be tough, independent, and emotionally guarded. They grew up hearing phrases like "boys don't cry," "man up," and "stop acting soft." These messages conditioned them to suppress their emotions rather than express them. But as we learn more about emotional health, it's clear that raising boys to be emotionally aware is just as important as teaching them strength.

Emotional awareness doesn't mean raising boys to be overly sensitive or fragile. It means teaching them how to recognize, understand, and manage their feelings in a healthy way. Boys who learn to express emotions constructively grow into men who communicate better, build stronger relationships, and handle life's challenges with more balance.

Take David, a father of an 8-year-old son, Jake. David was raised in a home where emotions weren't discussed. His father was present but distant, and the only acceptable male emotion was anger. Growing up, David struggled to express himself, often bottling up frustration until it came out in unhealthy ways. When he became a father, he realized he didn't want his son to go through the same thing.

One day, Jake came home from school upset because his friend had ignored him at recess. Instead of telling him to "shake it off" or "be a man," David did something different, he listened. He asked Jake what had happened, how it made him feel, and reassured him that it was okay to be upset. Then he helped Jake think of ways to handle the situation. That simple conversation showed Jake that emotions weren't something to be ashamed of, they were part of being human.

Raising emotionally aware boys starts with leading by example. Boys learn more from what they see than what they are told. A father who never expresses emotions teaches his son to do the same. But a father who talks about his feelings, who admits when he's frustrated, stressed, or even sad, shows his son that emotions are normal and manageable.

Encouraging open conversations is another key step. Many boys grow up believing that talking about emotions is something only girls do. Parents, teachers, and mentors can change this by creating a safe space where boys feel comfortable expressing themselves. Simple questions like "How was your day?" or "What was the best and hardest part of today?" can help boys open up.

Teaching emotional regulation is just as important as allowing boys to express their feelings. Being emotionally aware doesn't mean letting emotions take over, it means understanding them and responding appropriately. Instead of punishing a boy for getting angry, guiding him to take deep breaths, step away for a moment, or express himself with words helps him learn how to handle emotions in a healthy way.

Boys also benefit from seeing a variety of male role models. Coaches, teachers, older relatives, and family friends can all play a role in showing that masculinity and emotional awareness go hand in hand. When boys see strong, respected men openly expressing emotions, it challenges outdated beliefs about masculinity and helps them develop a more balanced understanding of what it means to be a man.

Breaking old patterns takes time, but the impact lasts for generations. Boys who grow up emotionally aware become men who are better partners, fathers, friends, and leaders. They have the confidence to express themselves, the strength to handle life's challenges, and the emotional intelligence to build meaningful connections.

David's small changes in how he spoke to Jake created a foundation that would shape his son's future. Instead of growing up confused about his emotions, Jake would understand them. Instead of suppressing his feelings, he would learn to understand them. Instead of feeling the pressure to "be tough" at all costs, he would know that true strength comes from self-awareness and balance.

A Word from the Author

Thank you for picking up Why are Men Expected Not to Cry. If this book helped you in any way, maybe it encouraged you to express yourself, rethink old beliefs, or simply feel understood. I'd really appreciate it if you could share your honest feedback on the site where you bought it.

Your thoughts help me and also help others decide if this book is right for them. I'd love to hear what part of it was most helpful to you.

www.ingramcontent.com/pod-product-compliance
Ingram Content Group UK Ltd.
Pitfield, Milton Keynes, MK11 3LW, UK
UKHW030728240225
455493UK00005B/458